WHITE NOISE
IN THIS WORLD
SILVER
IN THE NEXT

WHITE NOISE
IN THIS WORLD

SILVER
IN THE NEXT

POEMS

DANIEL ABDAL-HAYY MOORE

THE ECSTATIC EXCHANGE
PHILADELPHIA
2015

White Noise in This World Silver in the Next
Copyright © 2015 Daniel Abdal-Hayy Moore
All rights reserved.
Printed in the United States of America

For quotes any longer than those for critical articles and reviews,
contact:
The Ecstatic Exchange,
6470 Morris Park Road, Philadelphia, PA 19151-2403
email: abdalhayy@ecstaticxchange.com

First Edition
ISBN: 978-0-578-17287-3 (paper)
Published by *The Ecstatic Exchange*,
6470 Morris Park Road, Philadelphia, PA 19151-2403

Cover art by the author
Book formatting by the author
(based on Abdallateef Whiteman design and Yusuf Didona InDesign
instruction)
Back cover photograph © 2015 Mohamed Abraham

بسم الله الرحمن الرحيم

DEDICATION
To
Shaykh ibn al-Habib
(and the continuation of the Habibiyya
through Shaykh Dr. Abdalqadir As-Sufi
and Shaykh Moulay Hachim al-Belghiti)
Shaykh Bawa Muhaiyuddeen,
all shuyukh of instruction and ma'arifa,
Baji Tayyaba Khanum
of the unsounded depths

&

blessed wife Malika, at my side,
al-hamdulillah

*

*The earth is not bereft
of Light*

CONTENTS

INTRODUCTION

I should think a true book of poems would need no introduction. It would stand still in the dead center of everything like a shaft of light. Its existence both precedes it and echoes after it. The first one to utter in a new and indefineably mysterious usage of our everyday language, scrolled and embroidered in strange-sounding but beautifully soothing or majestically frightening ways, taking our hearts backward into prehistory and forward into the present perfect, that one is "reincarnated" each time anyone of us might say something that emits light and remains suspended in the air.

A poem is a linguistic screen that is also an amplifier to hear God's Voice about everything, and simultaneously at once. But that's putting the heart before the hearse. God's Voice has no screen. He needs no amplifier. Each gnat sings its trajectory. How a horse in a field here in Pennsylvania has a donkey friend browsing in the grass always nearby, for they are bonded in divine affection, and know each other's language.

In the middle or near the end of writing a new book of poems, *"With Every Breath,"* I suddenly began writing this one, but not in the usual 7"x10" Chinese High School notebook I've been buying for decades from the same shop in Philadelphia's Chinatown, black with red binding and trim, but in a little notebook, 4"x 6" inches. To let lines stack in a vertical rather than horizontal axis, with the intention to rise. Whose intention throughout is epiphany, to see into and past layers of literally everything in which we are (and which is also *in* us) drowned. Bathed in immanence and immediance. Echoing the vertical.

"White noise" is *"a random signal with a constant power spectral density,"* says Google. *"Such a signal is heard as a hissing sound, resembling the 'sh' sound in 'ash'. In music and acoustics, the term 'white noise' may be used for any signal that has a similar hissing sound."* After chemo and radiation my oncologist asked if I heard a hissing sound in my ears. I said no, having always thought of it as the Music of the Spheres. It's the background silence that is pure, whose purity is expressed as a "hissing sound." Not of snakes, but of bliss. Or the *whoosh* of the sacred perveyors of bliss. And in the Unseen Next World that's an inconceivable state, herein called "silvery."

God is in the lowest effects as well as in the highest causes

— William Blake

A poem is an egg

with a horse in it

— 4th Grader

TAKE ONE STEP FORWARD

Take one step forward
it all turns to light

But to pour from one
bottle to another

step back

At just the right balance
it pours itself

Whoever came from the
north in a light

jacket?

How did these
complex ships get

assembled inside the room?

Intricate machinery within
machinery

each cog going at its
own rate?

I write this as our
cat Lutfi drinks

water near my arm
from a plastic bowl

What gorgeousness
when nature is so

close to us!

I hear her lapping tongue
in her crouched silence

until she walks away

5/1

THE LAST THING I WROTE

The last thing I wrote
was *"the last thing I*

wrote"

Now it's time to bring the
cattle in

not for slaughter but for
laughter

We sit around playing
cards

the cows and me

They somehow get the
cards in the

clefts of their hooves

There's lots of ruminating
and chewing of cud

and that friendly cow
smell

At the edge of the world
these things occur

looking out over the
galaxies

where a cow dances
look! over the

moon and in the stars

Everywhere we look
these diamonds gleam

in us and outside us
as God intends

innumerable and pointing
always to the One in

all their dazzling
plenitude

with our sweet cow
breath

so smelling of wheat grass!

5/3

THE HEART IS A GOLD DISCUS

The heart is a gold
discus thrown from the

beginning of a life to the end
of each one of us

Tall trees whizz by

The history of the automobile
in slow motion

speeded up

The history of aviation
earthquake cycles

If the entire earth's population
were to smile one

smile once simultaneously
peace might

descend

As it is we're all
busy with our various

facial expressions
so the chance eludes us

and we're left with our
own scowls looking

back at us
from the mud

5/3

ONE DAY

One day all over the
world dogs started

eating their masters

while cats sat by and
watched

waiting for scraps

This is not a pretty idea

There was no shortage of
pet food for either

species

Even normally small and
delightful birds became

scavengers

The polluted seas had
risen and the

depleted forests gave up their
friendly ghosts

A miasma hung over the
world

What light there was
filtered to only a few

hardly enough to read by

Soft became hard and
hard cracked apart

God's Mercy still prevailed
and human consciousness

rose in a cloud

Worms took on the
business of cleanup

Roads were blocked by
ravenous beasts

All passwords were

annulled

A bright electricity
filled the air

Eyes watered over and
became blind

What solace remained
came in small

increments

Rivers returned to their
sources and their

sources ran dry

Shadows moved in the
darkness

and the darkness crouched
inside a single bead of light

God holds in His
Hands

5/3

THE TRUER ONES

The truer ones among us
have a golden pond

around their hearts
from which we can

drink to our heart's content

Although they move or
seem to move it's the

mountains behind them
moving through them

and their facial radiance
is more truly

the phases of the moon
and near-fatal

moments of eclipse

They sit in God's

inner courtyard
speeling yarns

Our hearts have
ears all over them

like a collage

What was the first
divine drip to drip

into us
begins to vibrate

and never stops from
then on

even among starlight
after the Big Bang

The truer ones among us
don't say much

which is saying a lot about
we who can't stop

saying

But they divide the
seas with the vertical

blade of their hand
and sew them together again

by pointing

Our heart's wounds
have the sutures

to show for it

God protect them
at the center and at the

peripheries

and permeate our spirits
with their bosom

companionship!

5/3

IN EVERY BREATH

In every breath
a face opens up

of such purity
whose radiance is

cornfields at their peak
moment of harvest

God's Face which is
no face we associate with

faces

coming over the hill at us
wherever and whenever

we happen to be
and overwhelmingly familiar

when we're
original emptiness

a worthy state for

contemplating God's works
inside and outside us

as has often been
iterated

But truly
the pigeon is a perfect

work of God

the fly a famous
confabulation that

we can't duplicate no
matter how hard

we try

And then there's air
itself and

churning seas

entering rainbow land and
coming out the other side

as fresh as a Spring shower

and the sparkle of the
freshly sprinkled

God's Face

Whose navigational pull
ordains the

saintly in us
a ladder of alchemical

gold with many rungs
that become one when

our heart's breaths
extend over canyons and

thoughts themselves
spark

ablaze with the
possibility of

vastness

Each gnat a
prince among gnats

Each bird the hoopoe of
Solomon

Each blink of our
eyes that *wali* of Allah

who could transport
Bilqis' throne in a

wink
then bring it

home again

5/3

WHAT DO ANY OF US

What do any of us
truly know?

How He ponders over the
entire universe

galaxy by galaxy

and if there's sentient
life there He

is their consciousness also
in each millimeter of

sentience each blink and breath
not different from our own

and on these wings we'll
fly there

by which I mean the
very words put down here

Pegasus ancestor of Buraq
for swifter realization

If you cry out
the stairwell will

disappear around you

and the field of gently
blowing grass goes

on and on

5/3

NOCTURNAL ANIMAL

I'm becoming a nocturnal
animal like the

owl that glides through the air

without making a sound

The dark is my cheeks and
its galaxies are my

lungs and my lungs are
this earth's oceans

endlessly pumping by
God's Magnetic Might

and its moonlight

and the rippling strip of light that
lays down on it like a

long-legged lover across a
shifting bed

Ah the world itself is
water constantly shifting

and all events just
evanescent reflections

passing through their ripples
in a forward spasm of

Divine energy

In this night also
like a box of darkness

lit to its four corners
from within

and distant trains sometimes
hoot across town and a car's

engine revs up a hill
a few blocks away

and murders and lovemaking
are committed on its

hills and in its valleys

and everyone speaks the secret
language of owls

whose wingspread flutters
with barely any motion

as they slide through seeming
nothingness after nocturnal

prey

Your whisper Lord
in the dark

5/4

HERE IN THE DARK

Here in the dark
you can just make out the

edges of the temple

A soft gong echoes up the
valley

A round white face is
just coming out from behind

its cloud as if to smile again

How many waves of silence
can leap up to our shore

then slide back again
into white noise?

If you can't face forward in the
dark it's unlikely you'll

move ahead when

daylight breaks its own

egg against its perfect edge

just as the
edges of the temple

are only a shade or two
darker than the

darkness itself
and you can just

make it out
in the dark

5/5

ROSES AND ECHOES

Roses and echoes

echoes of the rose

each petal a more
distant cry

out here where the
wind is rose-tinged

and each petal is
one of the Ninety-Nine

Names of Allah

The horse you ride is the
horse that will

carry you there

Its name is
Rose

5/5

CINCO DE MAYO

Richard Wagner sits on a
great stone

Which grows greater as
Wagner grows smaller

until he nearly
disappears

Seeping from the
base of the stone

colossally beautiful music

But this is not about
Wagner

I'm sitting out back in the
little patio garden first really

warm day the 5th of May
and between the passing

airplanes overhead and the

stereophonic birds' chirps

rotating around me
and a buzz saw down the

alleyway

and the lilt and cadence
of the air itself it

seems beween the *whooshes* and
silences

a silver invitation comes with a
distant cry

a dog bark becomes the
railers and nay-sayers

but the birdsong prevails above all
even as they pause to

preen or just pause to
look around

Consciousness is a

single eye in a
gold nimbus

that I just now
shut my eyes to see

The fact that I'm alive
and taking deep breaths

and seeing the ferns uncurl again
is a secret measurement in God's Care

a divine mathematics
of everything we do

Come to the birdbath you sparrows
unafraid of my presence

in your midst

Two workmen two doors
down are speaking Spanish

*How I'd love to
join their talk!*

5/5

THERE'S A BOX

There's a box on the road
that could hardly hold

the horse it holds
or the mezzo soprano

It could hardly come from
where it comes from

nor go to where it's going

It isn't going anywhere

A house and garden are
inside the box

A president and his cabinet
the cabinet bigger than the size of

a good size horse

The box whinnies

We would like to know
what's in the box

I've decided
I don't want to know

and I'm in the best
position to know

Let's leave the box
where it is

Now people are
upset with me

I've introduced a box
but kept it closed

as if I'm keeping a secret

Let's say there's a complete
down-to-the-last detail

galaxy inside the box
Let's say it's Allah's box

He's Creator and Keeper

Now do you mind if we
leave it unopened?

Here's a box
it could hardly hold the

earth it holds with its
moon and atmospheres

oceans full of micro-organisms
micro-organisms full of

even more microscopic
micro-organisms

Box within box within
box

It might even be the Kaaba
It sits in a rare light

You could even call it
Light within Light

5/8

TAKE THIS STRING

Take this string
and pull it taut

and you will see
what God has wrought

The flying serpent's
tail of fire

sets the cycles
to expire

over towns and
blackened streams

a stairway opens
in our dreams

the shadow of it
cuts across

like the haunted
albatross

This and every other
door

to go through to be
as before

5/14

SEWING NEEDLE

I picked up a sewing needle
and saw the

18,000 universes sliding in a
cloud of amber light through its

vertical eye

at either side dissolved
but when passing through the

needle's eye
bursting into song

every soul born
singing multitaneously

through

singing in between in the
eye's center

Singing the song of

Allah alone out the
other side

outlines now more
starlit from

within with our
soul's first faces

circulating across mountain peaks and
populations as

turgid as the seven seas

and Allah the One Divine
Eye

Who Sees
all

5/15 Miraj

A RUMMAGE SACK

A rummage sack
is all I've got

and in the sack
my cooking pot

and in my pot
a cooking hen

and in my hen
a delicious spread

to bring the local
magistrates

We'll sort the world out
state by state

and each of us will
have a pot

and that will be all
that we've got

with or without a
cooking hen

and that is all
Good day gentlemen

5/16

A FURLED UP VELOUR BLANKET

A furled up velour
blanket becomes for a

moment a black rose
at the foot of my

bed

A horse coughs and the
whole town notices

Layers of cloud above us
layers of cloud below us

Space all around us
for clouds to occur

The phone rings because
in some far-off universe

a magistrate fell asleep

while hundreds of giraffe

below run across the veldt

I spoke too soon
and the person I was

speaking to awoke

If you follow a smoke
trail it's unlikely you'll find

a snoozing dragon

All of this a zigzag
for God's Light to invade

and we roll around in it
like bubbles escaping from the

ocean's floor to pop on the
surface

in the sunlight
in never-ending

celebration

5/17

TO GO DEEP

To go deep
to look deep inside

you have to go to the
edge and look down

and not be afraid of the
party going on in there

They're all speaking your
language

Some in a lower
guttural form

some with the deferential
elegance of phrases

used before a Balinese king

but they're all yours
and though they try

they won't kill you

Talk nice to them
though sometimes you may

have to talk rough to the
gutturals

They don't respond to nice

and speaking of God and
repeating His invocation

has the power of a hundred
armies of nuns with rulers

clearing the board or at least
speaking over them

You may never drown them out
completely

but you can pipe them
down to near insignificance

with the help of Allah

5/20

TO PREPARE FOR DEATH

1) Love everyone
as if you mean it

2) *Mean it!*

3) *Really* mean it!

5/23

DEATH'S A LITTLE HUT

I think death's a
little hut you crawl into

that becomes too
small for you like

Alice with her head against
the ceiling and her

arms out the windows

and it's actually
cozier than life's

usual space all the
way to the outer

galaxies

Suddenly you fit yourself
exactly and that

fits into immortality's
fixed rectangle that

then expands to the
farthest limits

where planets whirl like
tops and galaxies like

music

Silver horses in stalls
waiting for their riders

Short mountains that upon
alighting shoot up to

impossible heights
giddier than actual

delight
alhamdulillah wa shukrulillah

Language out of love's
bubbling crucible

erupting

gloriously

nowhereward

5/25

LET DOWN YOUR GUARD

Let down your guard and
step among the

lily pads and the
stones

A wild light sprays up from
unexpected depths

Mouths appear at the
surface repeating His

ineffable Name that is
more like flowing water or

floating air

We can't go anywhere without it

nor anywhere without
Allah the Way and the

Guidepost shadow cast from
everything speaking in

perfect sentences

If our eyelids were our
lips our eyes would be

singing God's praises with
every glance

and every glance would
breathe from its own

center

fire upon fire and
space upon space

all the way out to our
innermost souls

No use to want wings
God's given us legs

and a secret whose
treasure has not only

already been opened but

already openly displayed as well

with every godly
glance we make

5/28

THAT WE'RE ALIVE AT ALL

That we're alive at all
is a miracle if you

think about it

We could have been born
the wheel on a cart

rolling down a hill

or a black fly in a
bottle buzzing for

all it's worth

or a cloudless sky
moving slowly westward

But we've been
born as we are

our smiles set crooked on our
moonlike faces

or in perfect symmetry

Our breaths both
bated and unbated

breathed through every
bend and curve

relaxed and
easy as we go

But we could have been
born the shadows

under an abandoned pier

or out at farthest sea
a giant squid

hiding in its depths

but we're not
we're these

light people

around a single knob of wisdom
one turn of which

would switch the world's lights on
once and for all

but only Allah knows
why and how

and how and why not

and we're best to
keep His secret from ourselves

in enlightened
delight

5/30

THE SPIRIT SAYS

The spirit says *Come*

the doors are open
and everyone's asleep

Here mountains rise
and clouds disperse

The body says *Let me*
gaze a bit longer

at pebbles on the
river bottom

The mind is a blind
photographer

Snap snap and the
images are caught

freeze dried and
categorized

When the doors are

shut again

we post them on the walls

But hurry
the animals are

assembling

The bird canopy
is forming into place

You take a
step and then

another

Are those insect wings
against your face

or the nerves of
nerviness?

To stand up against
the tide

to let the
kisses of the waters

lap your feet?

There's no normal
sun can warm you

after such a high
deluge

nor would you
want it to

As you stand you see
fish are

striving their way
home

As you gaze at the
trees you hear a

distant crack in the
heart of the forest

As you remain still
the heavens open

Your head now
high above the

clouds

5/30

IN THE PRAYER

In the prayer
our faces are

right up against it

standing still in God's
acres eyes open and

downcast or slitted
half shuttered

at precipice edge
toes at the knife blade of it

facing where the Kaaba is
in front or way far away in

front

There's a special air that
brushes our faces

hands at peace

legs holding us up in space

hearts on their offering pedestals
before His Cosmic Glory

visible only in the
depths of our souls

where their whistling can be
heard each

galaxy piping its own tune
colossally played in

close harmony

and we in ours
as milky as our

mothers' breasts each
doubled billion of them

since time began

6/1

THE JEWEL

The jewel worn by the
most elaborate potentates

who've sent their
expert divers down or their most

intrepid miners deep into the
earth to find

and that laid on black velvet
dazzles the whole room making

the most brilliantly radiating
showcases to

pale in comparison

Here it is! Located right

where Allah put it at
birth

between our ribs

between our selfish selves and our

better natures
guarded over by angels

worn on the outside as
well as the inside

gracing the headdresses of the most
elegant elephants

This *"jewel of great price"*
this diamond in the

rough experience itself
cuts to its most

exquisite facets

a knife no harder known than
our struggling and striving

able to slice mountains and
moons in two

in imitation of our
Prophet peace be upon him

whose own heart jewel
illumined both heavens and

earth

in one glance and one
reverberant heartbeat

forever
ameen

6/7

A SAINT

A saint the
size of your thumbnail

rides the steed the
size of Aldabaran

that configuration of
stars nestled in the

hilly bosom of
intimate discourse

we say and do not
say

we indicate best by
passing entirely away

so those stars show
and the mountains of

space behind them
not seen except with the

naked eye

The plain is littered with
lovers such as

this infinitesimal
saint

Each breath of
theirs

last or always
next to last

is the pulse of the world
and the zipper that

zips and unzips the

surf of every beach
on every ocean

The steed throws back its
head and new suns

explode

How can we continue with such
heady stuff?

There must be a way
out of here

that isn't
quite so bright!

6/9

GRAY FOX

for Tom Clark

A gray fox this time
with black nose

slips almost unnoticed
along the city street

next to the great woods

and most think he's a
neighborhood cat out for a

serendipitous stroll

a few sardine cans whose
oils may not be completely

ingested

He's slick in the
full moonlight

as if wearing ermines

the light off his
gray coat shines

and he's thinking foxy
thoughts pretty

unfathomable to such as

we with our limited but
technologically supported

communication skills

The fox who yips and
barks at night so

neighbors think it's a
dog fight or a

tomcat commotion

bouncing along
nose choosing from the

menu of odors we can't
even smell

Stops
pricks up his ears for a

moment
stock still

momentarily majestic

then ambles on
as much in God's

sight as we are only
Oh so much more

naturally glamorous!

6/12

I REALLY DIDN'T THINK

I really didn't think I'd
be alive this summer

— and here I am
alive!

6/13

THE CURLED AND THE UNCURLED

The curled and the
uncurled

The leavened and the
unleavened

Alternate ribbons laid out on
sand

grain by grain

The top of the planet
the bottom of the planet

as if spun on a pivot

The sheer and the
dense

The see-through and the see
nothing

The pre-event and the

post-event

The shadow and the
substance

Edges and centers
ulteriors and

exteriors unguilefully

displayed

We carry a giant
pane of window glass

shouting *"Vitrines! Vitrines!"*

The loose and the
tight

What perishes
what persists

ultimately and
forever

Never more than a delicate
wisp in the

first place

us and our every
precious breath

hopping away from us like those
tiny red

Amazonian frogs

Tall night over
everything

Jubilant day
burst forth

never diminishing

even as its moisture
dries to a crisp

sunlight stretched

everywhere

and the holiest holy
darkness

Flesh of our flesh
in this

endless festivity

sealed in God's wink
before we can

think it
us being that wink at

least

while the rest belongs
entirely to God

6/13

SOMETIMES THE SWEETNESS

Sometimes the sweetness is
so intense we

burst into tears for no
reason

A house full of windows
sailing along catching

sunlight in every one

Roads going nowhere
under a canopy of

sparrows

Drinking water that suddenly
turns to wine

And we stand unsteadily
perfectly sober on

one foot or many

like an astrolabe at

high sea calculating our
deft hypotenuse

to reach shore

Sometimes the light around here
and inside here

is so brilliant
bees make a beeline in the

barn's high window
and out they swarm

to a lone tree by a
rushing green river somewhere

making their honey even more
furiously joyous than

before

We can't stand it

nor to be without it for

long

We weren't guaranteed it
and when it shivers down

through us
thank the Giver

and let the gift go

and we along with it!

6/16

OUR BODIES

Our bodies are time

Time is ticking

Our bodies are the
clock

6/16

WAS THAT A GUNSHOT?

Was that a gunshot
heard across the city

or just angels dropping
furniture again?

Are those gathering clouds
of charcoal tinged

puffiness

or angel thoughts
massing and

unmassing in the sky?

Are we waiting at this
edge to get at

least a glimpse of the
next

that angle other

more than that

other angle

The shadow thrown
athwart

where flying things
hang suspended where they

happen to be in space

until angels change their
minds and let the

dross go and keep the
gold to shine with

silver

Are these words to express
the ineffable

or to only show the
empty space where it

takes place?

The catch in the
throat and how the

eyes tear up at its
pearl-shaped

manifestation while also generating
an imperishable music

Oceans have nothing on it
they only slurp its

edges

It lifts up like Sayyedina
Sulaiman's carpet

over the city and its
gunshots and its

gunshot wounds
and its bullets penetrating

clear to the
other side

6/16

AURORA BOREALIS

Would the Innuit live to
wear his new

coat of seal fur?

Would the moose live to
swagger a bit with that

rack of antlers?

Would I live to wear the
vest that fits so perfectly

with all its useful
pockets and flaps and

almost invisible
silent zippers?

Would the Spring arrive again on
time after winter

living through itself and its

green urgencies

till Summer?

Would the clouds one day form
readable sentences on their

own or disperse into various
wayward puffs as usual

into the general atmosphere?

Would this poem live to be
read by at least one

living person
who might tuck it onto one of his or

her own vest pockets and ride
out on his or her

icy toboggan over the living
tundra in search of the

most glorious
aurora borealis?   6/18

THE MONTH

The month is drawing to a close
and it's only just begun

The ducks are falling out of
line they're so confused

I think things are
taking longer and hardly

any time has passed

Then I look at my life
this rugged terrain of

crags and plains
under an eternally

pink sky

and the planet chorus
humming out there

in left field

They don't seem in a
hurry

The ants in the
bathroom sink

are just looking

I admit to changing their
destiny from time to

time not out of
blood lust but to

discourage wholesale
immigration

Sounds like America
I'm *in* but not *of*

America just as I'm
in but not *of* time?

Well I don't think we can
say this about us and time

That poem three poems
back can tell you that

but even things like
icebergs these days

seem to be in a hurry

Are there no roses left anywhere
to stop and smell?

I'm not lamenting the culture of
expendables and temporal

onrush

God's waters pour as they
pour all praise each

moment

and the small house of our
next habitation

draws ever closer

There are those slow
skies above us

and Allah the Center of
all to hold onto

in time or out of time

amen

6/19

AN ANGEL SLICED

An angel sliced into
several pixels

becomes several angels

and their fabulous
jubilant wings

fill the sky
in several slices

so that with each breath of ours
several more scintillant

beings transpire
and when we inhale

our inward skies reflect
this sheer abundance

multiplied by the score-fold

until really we're in a

constant upward and outward shower

of angelic susurrations
in all directions

the way sea creatures exist
in the sea

surrounded by the ever-shifting
element that sustains them

with all ocular and aural
perspectives in a constant

fanning outward and inward
our own selves

dissolved in the abundance

a sheen of airy nothingness
a trillion angelic sighs of

sheer existence before Allah
in ever constant

gratitudinous encirclings
wheel within wheel

infinitely pursued

to the axel of His Love
whose oiled whisper keeps this

reality spinning
ever more multitudinously

6/20

STARFISH

Is starfish clinging to a
rock in a tide pool

any more or less a
salient feature of this

planet than say a
billionaire sitting in his

or her solarium sipping
cognac?

A tide goes in and a
tide goes out on

both at about the same
rate

a certain twinkle
submerged for a time of

watery contemplation
suited to each subject

On mortality if that's one's
concern over all others

or just a certain newness of the
thereness for both

starfish and billionaire in this
planetary sphere and

hothouse for all our
actions and for our

innermost consideration of
them

to oneself and others and to
God

and the biggest tide of
all is coming in

and will just as
easily go out

6/25

BRING THE MOON

Bring the moon a little
closer so I can

see your face

This corner in the all-night
diner is in shade

I looked for you among the
fresh carnations

next to the booth's jukebox
selector

all the songs on it
silent

all the customers
mute

The diner goes on for
miles in

dazzling aluminum padding
and the silence of the grave

Our record gets selected
falls onto the turntable

and after a prelude of
scratches

plays its mournful
tune

an old standard older than
the vision out the

window of long trucks in the
dust of time

rusting into monoliths

The night is turning silver
as the gold of day

draws near

The wheel we're on

knows no corners

but spins smoothly
in a noble silence

in every circumstance

and the pop tune
whistling in our ears is

white noise in this world
silver in the next

The hallelujah chorus
in the strangest places

The straw we sip the
divine soda through our

God-given bodies
imbibing His blessings

straight

6/27

THE FEEL OF A T-SHIRT

The feel of a T-shirt
being put on over the

upper body as it
flutters down

might be what it
feels like to be a

fish going through
water

6/29

SOMETHING GHOSTLY

There's something already
ghostly about us as we

go through the
material world

We pop up here or there
fade into the background

our tentative off-again on-
again relationships

somewhat evasive
often elusive

feeling we're not quite
here

Our sleeping then waking then
sleeping again

even awake

How we know through it all

Allah has greater
reality than we do

Ours a reflected light
circulating in our

ghostly orbits
even without

fluttering

6/29

ON A LAKE

On a lake as large as
heaven the

ducks are as tiny
as dots

Whoever let the rank air into this
perfect perfection?

A thief with rainbow
gauze over half his

face who walks
sideways and takes

daylight with him

But just one window thrown
up in wonder

scatters the butterflies

until they form again

around the sleeping maiden's

face

All the old fables and tales
have made the front

pages of our un-modern world

All the final adumbrations

the five alarm fires

of the heart
and the poorest heart's rejoicings

When we lift our eyelids beyond their
usual frames

we notice green vineyards
that go on into the indefinite

for miles beyond what
human eyesight can

encompass

and angels' song is most
pleasant under a

tree you've planted yourself from a
sprig from the sidewalk

and the *hooing* and *wooing* that
goes on in their domain

filtering down through the
branches of that

tree in excited
birdsong

7/9

LINES OF DEFENSE

The first line of defense
against a dissolving world is

let it dissolve

The second line of defense is
wear a tight-fitting

hat the size of a
thimble

and be lost in it

The third line of defense really is
have nothing whatever to

do with it either way
letting it or not letting it

go

Its way and our way
are not the same way

We live in the heartbeat of a
lightning bolt

and the world lives in a
threat of storm that

often turns into one
and nothing remains

While with this
third way

we remain in God's
domain and

always will

as the world goes down
below the

windowsill

7/9

HOW SWEET TO DREAM

How sweet to dream
in the summer heat

inconsequential reveries and
dreams

to go to the reassembled imagery
haunting the inner cavern at a

single snap of the heart's finger
against its glass walls

One ping and decade's old
pictures come to life

with their erotic charge
as if we're in an

air balloon lifting ever so
softly and high through the

projected memories
taking new pictures of them again

and reprojecting them against a great
incorporeal screen

who may stay longer alive than
we do

either as our eternal flesh around
the next world's ethereal light

or else they disappear like old skin off the
soul's snake as we

enter eternity all
wingedly buoyant and

facing forward to God's
incandescent embrace

7/10

BLUE MARBLE

I live in a blue marble
on a blue marble

in space

Walk down blue lanes
in a blue house

alongside a black river
whose water is

clear as glass

amid breezes from
blue trees

thinking these
blue thoughts

The lens we see through
is the glass we've been

given
we wash clear

under a blue stream

In moonlight all this
blue turns to gold

in golden moonlight
God's outline can just be

made out light by light
in a shining space

in the blue night

O may we come to You
with what we've

got Lord

for only You can turn it
into its original

silver

Only You
can make it

right   7/10

AT SOME POINT

Vision perceives Him not, but He perceives [all] vision; and He is the Subtle, the Aware.
(Surah al-An'aam: 103)

At some point you
have to decide just

how much you want an
entirely new perception of things

as they are

We're not going to find God
in a threadbare overcoat

in a dank laboratory
down a zigzag street on a

moonlit night in
Vienna

Who turns to us nevertheless
with a most radiant smile —

but in everything and nothing

there and *there* and *there*

The songbird never alights too
long on any branch

until it plans to sleep
there

It's all to do with
radical simultaneity

or as the Buddhists say:
"Interdependent Arising"

of neon green farmland going on
for miles

fringed with willow copses
under bright blue sky

firefly on the carpet
blinks its thanks when

returned back outside

Nothing reveals Allah more

than His invisibility

though *"The Invisible One"* is not
one of the Ninety-Nine Names of

God

nor is *"The Visible One"*
but only

"He Who Sees"

7/15

CHANCES ARE

Chances are
there's not much time to

lasso the wind horse
before the whole hillside

goes up in blazes

Of course we live forever
but there's a measurement here

of divine mortality
whose every second is a

flock in flight of

extinct passenger pigeons
carrying messages from

extreme distance to
extreme nearness

The tangible eludes us

because of the
jealousy of the intangible

for His sake and Good
Pleasure

We sacrifice the one for the
other

through our unflagging diligence
in remembering Him

as He goes His ways
within us

and we turn inside-out to
see Him

7/15

YOU'VE GOT TO ADMIRE

You've got to admire the
puff of smoke the

evanescent thought

They make their play
and evaporate

disappear off the
face of the earth

A thunderstorm's arrived
with its jailors

jangling their lightning-bolt
keys

Whatever disembodied being gets itself
enough together to present

itself in perfect

reproduction of the

real thing

Thing is: *nothing's real*
except He Who made and

continues to stand by it
looking through eyes that are not

eyes

and speaking with
tongues that are not

dragons in the heavens
or any such thing

and Who so
perfectly embodies

disembodied-ness

whose key and secret belongs to
He Himself the

whole time

7/16

TINY BUG

About to take off
this tiny bug

has more faith
than entire nations

It throws itself
wings whirring

out into the air

until it lands
somewhere

Ministers and magistrates
might do as well

as this tiny mite smaller than
the whitish crescents

at our fingernails' cuticles

we don't know what if

anything it's thinking

Does it imagine a
destination and then just

go there?

Does it even know
we're watching?

It has no apparent
character in itself but is a

perfect example of its
species

though it may have a
somewhat more

crooked mandible smile or
antenna jauntily tilted say

than the next one

as it sails perfectly oblivious

to these ruminations

to a safe landing
elsewhere

7/16

ONLY ALLAH

I was born in a hospital in
Alameda California

Only Allah

I had this face I
have even now

Only Allah

The lights crisscrossed
this way and that

Only Allah

My parents loved each other
and showed affection

Only Allah

I drew pictures on
construction paper

Only Allah

The door swung open and
I went through it

Only Allah

Sat as a Buddhist
facing a wall

Only Allah

Wrote *Dawn Visions* on a
trip to Mexico

Only Allah

San Francisco
1964

Only Allah

Angel Gabriel
stood up in a tree

Only Allah

The Floating Lotus
Magic Opera Company

Only Allah

A Sufi shaykh's
deputy in an

attic room in Berkeley

Only Allah

Shaykh ibn al-Habib
in Meknes Morocco

Only Allah

Clouds rolled away
and keep rolling away

Only Allah

Drove with five others

in a Pugeot in Algeria

Only Allah

Met saints of Allah there
Hajj Isa ben Hajj Isa and Hajj Isa

Only Allah

Married Malika in a
burst of light

Only Allah

Came to Philadelphia
where Bawa's gaze covers us

Only Allah

The *Deen* of Islam a garden
with living vegetation

Only Allah

Shaping us into

alchemical human beings

Only Allah

Cancer *zamzam* hemp oil
wheat grass

Only Allah

The Door of Light
with a Dark Door inside it

Only Allah

The Door of Dark
with a Light Door inside it

Only Allah

Being here for a moment
going on forever

Only Allah

*La ilaha illa Allah
Muhammad Rasulullah*

BEWARE THE HORSE

Beware the horse that
doesn't neigh

the goat that
doesn't bleat

the fish that won't
wiggle its dorsal

the cow that won't jump
o'er the moon

This land is irregular
and its fences zigzag

Clouds are heavy
but never rain

We live between two
dusts in perpetual storm

the one of our birth
and the one how we'll be

when the future makes good its
one certain promise

prestidigitation that doesn't
betray its methods

occasionally doing the
unthinkable in its

defense of the undoable

But we don't await just
this world's justice

in the rockslide of light that
covers us

7/21

QUIET DESPERATION

Here in the Baltimore Aquarium
a lot of fish are

leading their lives
but not I think in

quiet desperation

while a lot of people
are watching them

bob and swim

in various states of
awareness here in the

air element where things
crawl walk fly and

fall with lungs so
sweetly adapted we could

if God had willed

go on here forever

like these endlessly bobbing
jellyfish with their

sublime inaudible music

7/21

SILVER ROSE

Allah in Qur'an says He
constructed the world

with one command

You can see it sizzle along
into being right down to the

pin on the table in
front of you

shining in the
sun

Rocks skies logs waters
hairs bacteria railroads

cells cars headlines
backstairs wells

You can see how everything
comes alive at once

little threads with LED lights
running through everything from that

simple command every millisecond
everything deflated and inflated

over and over

and we too
making our strange way

through the thickets
to the oval rose garden way

inside it all

where a single bush grows
by that same command

on which one silver rose blows
before it goes golden

7/25

THE MOON

The moon brought people
home for dinner and

shone on them until
they were done

The ocean washed ashore
got up went into

town ordered a
custom-made

suit but found it
wouldn't fit

and never would

The night grew
afraid of the dark

and so had stars tell it
stories to calm its

fears

All the mighty elements
mixed together the

best they could
some meshing others

repelling

until this world
snapped back to itself

with us inside it

guiding its workings against any
self-destructive tendencies

until it was able to
get along on its own again after

its basic trauma of
ever-metaphorical being

while God's Light plays

core and essence of

everything that exists
reflected back to itself in

His mirror

enclosed in the
brambles of our hearts

7/27

THERE'S A DONKEY

There's a donkey up ahead
on the horizon that could be

said to be our lives

keeping its head down
bearing its weight

flicking its ears at any
sign any signal of

life beyond itself
a humble image suitable to our

arrogance our
pervasive self-conceit

We with our patch of grass
demanding a whole pasture

with our rainbow of sky
demanding an endless

blue that fills a canyon

We with our part in the
ocean itself with all our

watery wish-washiness

and our celestial pulse
pushing shoreward in froth

and pushing out from it again

back to the central vastness
whose main corridors are lit for

whales

while up ahead the donkey pauses
not unsure of its way

but to listen for cues
as to how to go on in

any direction to get to its

goal

and then wanders off into
God's fields and loses all

sense of anything completely
being embraced by His more

spectacular and sacredly circular
orbit forever

instead of just endlessly
around and around

seeing now with more than
donkey eyes

out of that thoughtful
donkey face rather than

in the worldly sun

8/1

THE DANCE OF THE THREE-TOED SLOTH

The dance of the three-toed sloth
as well as the

dance of the hummingbird

The dance of rocks on a
rock-strewn hillside

as well as stockbrokers
streaming along

Fleet Street

The dance of atoms in a
ray of moonlight

as well as
the dance of the thoughts of a

two-year-old just now
delighted by soap bubbles

These interlocking circles
above and below the

circles we see in our
eyes wherever we look

here and there and
back again

The dance at the tip of a leaf
as well as the slow cold dance of the

rest of the iceberg we can't see

all in continual motion
on the dance floor of

God's continuous ocean

8/1

HE LEANED OVER

He leaned over
and light poured out of his

eyes
like sand

Granules of light

8/5

A DROWSY NUMBNESS

A drowsy numbness
o'ertakes me

sitting on a bench that says
"Be at rest, poet"

in the Morris Arboretum
Philadelphia

in the shade really
hot sun all around me

and a bank of rowdy
blackeyed susans in a

grassy bed in front of me

Where are my cool angels of
wind and rain

hidden in the air
like letters slipped into

envelopes

that dissolve right

before our eyes
into unlikely zebras

bounding away
to all the mechanical

sounds overheard even here in
placid Morris Arboretum

August seventh
twenty-fifteen of the

year of our Lord
within the Lord of our

Lord deeper in than even
any Lordly deepness in the

deepmost eternal quiet
way inside this moment

*(except for a squeaky
bird squawk from*

somewhere over there)   8/7

IF A WHITE OWL

If a white owl is
surrounded by a

white frame of light

or a black panther
held in the embrace

of the blackest of night

or a red fox suddenly
engulfed in flames

and our names suddenly
flew free of us into

a sky so perfectly blue

we might not end up
knowing exactly who we are

blending our
nothingness into the

bright nothingness all
around us

and only our eyes awake
to know who we are

by our seeing

God's corrective lenses
in front of our hearts

to focus His Light

Then owl and panther
would stand out in

bold relief from their
own anonymous selves

in which His deepest light
dwells

8/11

I STILL GO TO SLEEP

I still go to sleep
from a state of

consciousness

The Prophet said his
eyes slept but his

heart stayed awake

What could that be?

Each snowflake on a
Swiss rooftop?

Each glitter on an oily
lake?

Each dark cloud passing in the
white sky?

His consciousness was not
like our consciousness

and yet like a window
partakes of what it

sees by having been
seen through

we have a portion in the

Prophet's consciousness
that Allah's given us

like a telescope or a
microscope to

see though

and whose vehicle to
get there is

constant remembrance of
Allah

Whose process is our
goal

leaving nothing out
in any conscious way

in the ever-awakened
fields of love

8/12

THE DECREE OF ALLAH

The decree of Allah has a
way of catching

up with us

Or from another
direction a way of

surprising us on the
way to it by its

very flower-like
unfoldings

petal by
painful petal

like an unfolding
flower of flames

whose crackle at our

ears wakes us
up

a crackle like
civilizations crumbling

their pillars falling
inward

or a bonfire on a beach
watching its sparks

meander up into blackness

It steps toward us
one sparkling glance at a

time

It brandishes no
weapons but its

face at first is
unrecognizable

except in full sunlight

and even then the
subsidiary beasts

in all gentleness

take off in flight into the
depths of the golden

forest of its origins

How can mortals withstand
such sudden shocks?

The tectonic plate of
God's decrees on us

is filled with sweetmeats
and delicacies wrapped in

edible foils

Look at God's Light
as it expands past the

bud into full flower
under the single silvery drop

of His implacable
shower   8/15

BREAK ALL THE RULES

Break all the rules but one:
That you follow the rules

Kick all the dogs but one:
the dog of desire

Look over the fence at
the neighbor's

yard if the neighbor's
yard *is your soul*

And if the dog of desire is for God
the dog of the Cave

feed that dog choice
premium cuts

If that rule is the
Straight Path to Him

only break it to mend it
at a deeper level

and go there as a
pauper begging for

bread

and if that bread is gold
eat it in health

for it's worth its weight in
wheat

and the rain that sprouts it is
your tears of sweet desperation

and your tears of joy
are a herd of yellow

horses riding in blue surf

and all the riders are
yourself atop each

yellow horse of God's Light
splashed by an ever-greater

brightness   8/15

I STRIVE TO STAY

I strive to stay in the
treetops where the

birds are

and the sunlight

that thunders
among the leaves

each twitch in the
breeze another stanza

of the ocean-sky's
outpouring

8/15

LIKE A SUDDEN PINK EXPLOSION

Like a sudden pink
explosion in the

depths of the sea

but black that deep where
no light comes

and attended in the
dark by schools of

dazzling rainbow fish with
blue faces but also

black in that darkness

and surrounded by
mysterious currents

invisible in the water
but capable of carrying

tons of whales

in the dim deeps

our hearts mostly
unbeknownst to us

do their work of
healing to

themselves and
others

8/16

WE'RE THE ALIVE ONES

We're the alive ones
while we're alive

but when we die
others will mourn us

others will have to
put us to rest

The Prophet's Companion
Abu Dharr

God bless him
at the end of his life

is said to have traveled with a
goat to pay for

someone to bury him
since the Prophet said to him

"You will die alone"
peace be upon him

In the compass of our
consciousness

this is almost inconceivable

We look out from a
living core

but when we die
others have to

bury us
as others will have

to bury them
in turn

8/18

THERE'S A BIRD

There's a bird
of more than exquisite beauty

whose single feather
more than covers the world

whose eye alone
has all the galaxies

for moisture

who's traveling at
supersonic speeds

whose unearthly cry
is the sound existence makes

moving through the sky
whose entire size is a

drop of light
sitting on God's finger

that pointing
creates

you and I

8/21

GIVE UP SEARCHING

Give up searching through
books and following clues

The pot of molten gold is
already tipped at the

top of your cliff

and as its waterfall
splashes across you

eyes look neither out nor in

everything shows its
intimate crystal

Light is faceted into its
rainbow constituents

and all our faces lose their
mask-like surfaces

to show the

radiant candle going through its

continuous metamorphosis
charging the lights from

here to Madagascar
and back again

8/25

THE LAND OF NOD

The Land of Nod
or from the mirror side

The Land of *Don*

(even with a motorcycle blustering
by on the back alley

and its driver with guzzling power
mightily vibrating under his

crotch

going off to a destination
all his own

as noisily as possible)

The Land of Dreamy Nodding
opens up like a tall

wheat field by Van Gogh
you can wade through with

wheat tassels tickling your elbows

and there's nothing else like it anywhere
you're suddenly totally free

even to fly if that should be
with no need of vehicular conveyance

other than holding your
arms out occasionally to

correct your balance

and then the next door neighbor dog barks
and it's this world again

with its distant leaf blower or
weed whacker discouraging the

silence with its
guttural snickering

And your eyelids ache a
little for a bit more

nodding in this 87° heat
at the dwindling of August

All this wide-open space
and all of us the

sentience it can hold
plus a zillion others

above sea level and
down in the sea's depths

all of us from
potentate to jellyfish

going forward only
to our destinations reserved for

us alone

holding or not holding an
unquenchable heart's candle for

he Whose only single Sentience
abides

with the roar of a
lion or two

and a peacock's
raucous cry

putting a period at the
end of it

in the all-encircling
stillness

8/25

THERE'S A MOVIE

There's a movie a mile high
running inside us

playing all the atmospheres
all the great historical

skirmishes and broken treaties
all the romances

It runs continuously

We even make an
minor appearance in a

supporting role
or as my theatrical debut in first grade

we carry a cardboard tree
and hold very still

Sometimes the movie
flows all around

its ends meeting in a
kiss before us

Apaches burst through the screen
or the screen goes suddenly

blank

Ah the blank screen of the
movie inside us that

causes some if not
all our anxieties

when we could settle down
to enjoy miles of

silveriness and shining
light

no longer flickering to us its
strobe-light brightness

until a tiny fern appears
that morphs into a

forest

a vast dark forest
full of creatures

8/27

RUNNING WITH THE WILD ARMADILLOS

Running with the wild
armadillos!

*Well actually I'm not
but I love the*

idea of it

And anyway armadillos
don't run they

snuffle
or when alarmed

curl up into a ball
an armor-plated

ball

*But I'm running with the
wild armadillos*

on our way to Allah

It's a gravelly terrain and
you never know for sure what's

happening

Little underbrush and less
water

but ambrosia at the end

for those of us
running

armadillos and me
plus badgers and ostriches maybe

and our dear friend
the kangaroo

But this all ripples in the
wind like a good

painted backdrop should

revealing a light

being pulled

forward and forward
in time's slide-whistle

to a shore with no
edge

and a horizon that
doesn't touch

the earth

So let's take an
armadillo under each arm to the

starting line and at the
next gunshot of breath

start running in breath or
out of breath

the goal having spread out
everywhere

scintillant with sunshine's stars

aglitter in our eyes to see

God's brilliance
radiating

all around us

8/27

SAVE THE UMBRELLA

Save the umbrella for the
one who's drowning

Save the motorbike for the
singer who's singing

off key

Save the world itself
for the children of

children

Not all of us can fit inside
an egg shell to be

born anew

Save the sad songs for the
whales as they

lament and pine deep down
in the deep

Save lilting melody for the
lover visiting his beloved's

balcony

Save a gourmet meal for the
brand new Panda bear mother

so long as it's bamboo shoots
in butter or better

right from the ground

If we don't turn into
flying creatures before the

next full moon
save us some shoes

for walking on the earth again
after our exhilarating

stroll sometimes in the
air and

sometimes not

This won't last forever so
someone dance at the end

It's always better to go out
dancing with the

Friend

8/28

THE FIRST BET

The first bet is the
better betting the

second better won't
bet

but the second better
had better bet or the

first better will win the
bet

The two betters
having betted

now face the better
better's greatest bet

since only one of the two
betters can possibly

win the bet

But the second better has
secretly bet the

first better's bet would
lose the bet

so the second better
can better the

first better by
winning the first bet

bettering the first
better by being so much

better than the first
better by betting and so

winning the bet

8/29

ALL THE MULTIFARIOUS

All the multifarious loves pouring
past us in their

continuous stream

with their giant "O"s of halos
puffing into the sky as if from

giant cigars

Passion that took
hold of us and

shook us down to our
shins

A bridge flung in fairy lights
over nothingness

We climbed walls on
ladders of skin

and eyes watched us
as we rose

not higher perhaps but
laboriously deeper

If the mask slips
God's behind it with His

oceanic vista
singing out over the

blackest waters

It's no good turning away from this
for without love's heart-broke turnstiles

we can't get onto divine
tracks

and love's sublimity elude us

9/4

A QUIET BUG

A quiet bug walks discreetly
behind a bottle on my

bathroom sink

taking it a little slow
to not attract attention

when I turn on the
light

9/4

AH!

Ah!
that explains it

Trees are held up by
giant webs of

star net

interstellar telephone poles
redwoods and cedars

And squirrels chasing
up and down their

looming trunks are the
systems' operators whose

twitch whiskers
transmit galactic messages

Reflections are actually
the same universe

inside the water

got to by secret passageways
not by diving in

same people doing the
same thing upside-down

to us

This world comes up to a
solid barrier you can

only cross by dying
simple or fancy

whatever God's Decree

No one can slip under the
tent flap

But some dissolve away significantly
to taste and live in the

other side's atmosphere
while still smiling and

nodding on this side

for anyone who
meets them

Which explains
their perfect equilibrium

and the state of not really being
affected much by the

goings on of this world
while yet in

perfect sympathy
with it

and God's Merciful rain falls on
all of us

which explains why
no matter what

state we're in
all of us

get wet

9/5

OF THE STONES

Of the stones along the road
there's one I've

held before

It's flat and round and
smooth

and gives me great
satisfaction to rub it

Maybe it's my mother's breast

Maybe it's the stone
thrown into the pond

that started my unwinding

Or of such unearthly
smoothness it somehow

reminds me of Allah

Of this world and

not of this world

hard but soft to the
touch

The very swollen curvature of
caress

Its smoothness
invites me into heaven

I might take it up and
skip it across these

dark and light dappled
waters myself

whether or not it
reaches the other shore

I put it back on the
white beach where I

found it

It disappears

into the whiteness

and I feel no
regrets

I feel fulfilled

One smooth stone out of
so many

meant for me alone

9/7

ROTATING FAN

I've turned the
rotating fan up a

notch faster

It swings across like a
sentry

back and forth forcing hot
air to curl away in

rolling arabesques

globulous waves
invisible patterns

no doubt glorious to
see in their natural

flow made now so
more agitatedly

gladsome

instead of a more
and more oppressive

flat hot blanket on
top of me

accompanied by fan
music as of very

distant airplanes
readying for takeoff

and me their single
passenger hoping for a

bit more sleep
in the graceful godly

froths of its cooler
bosom

9/9

AN ANIMAL THAT CONTAINS

An animal that contains
all animals

with or without tusks and
ferocious feet

eyes like semaphores

A human that contains
all humans

powerless and placid
harmonized with

God and everything surrounding
both outwardly and

inwardly

On a planet that contains
all planets and

planetary bodies

in perfect circulation

around a perfect sun

that contains all
solar systems so deeply

far flung

No breath taken that doesn't
contain all breaths

No glance that doesn't
take in that far line of

trees so staunchly
standing up the hill

That mountain range that
contains all terrains

This sky that contains all skies
and this eye

that contains all eyes

seeing only Allah Who
is not and

is
all things to which

all else is
nothing

9/11

THERE'S A SOUND

There's a sound in my
ears and the

low hiss of a pilot light

one swirling left the other
sizzling right

Their latitudes make the world
though the world rolls

away from here into both
day and night

with their seeming
solidities and solemnities

as close as China

as far away as Mars

in this ever-hopeful
consciousness of ours

willing to walk miles along
barbed wire to some idea of

freedom
that word that sits

unrhymed in all our
hearts

deluding some
liberating some

under this peculiar
atmospheric dome

we call home

God's call to us
being all

His Divine Zone
our flesh and

bone

9/17

THE STATE OF ABANDONMENT

The state of abandonment is
almost too much to bear

finding Allah in it
harder to achieve

The air around us the same
but our hearts have sunk

Old memories of the earliest facts of it
the first time felt and recalled

make us want to
go down into the

well of it and
cry our eyes out

back to the childhood
trauma of it

when there was no
railing of safety to

grip onto

and the universe was
whizzing by without us

enjoying what was denied to us
by a simple insouciance

in our direction
by our parents or peers

They took my older brother with them
on a car trip to the

Grand Canyon
and when they me asked what they could

bring back for me
I thought some

rocks for a rock collection
like the next-door neighbor boy had

in elegant profusion in a special
room on top of his garage

with ultraviolet light
that made the quartzes

dazzle a dark ethereal
purple

They left me with another
neighbor boy my first friend

Arthur

for a week or two
and when they got back

they'd bought a kind of
inverted shoebox cover with some

small rocks glued onto it
with typed out labels underneath

my parents had got
by the side of the road

mentioning how it was
"real Indians" who sold it to them

Just now the abandonment feeling
rushed back to me

having just awakened not
knowing at first where my

wife was
back to five or six years old

looking at some punky rocks
glued to a cruddy shoebox lid

(it probably came from China)

in the dark basement
where I kept them

9/17

A HUNDRED AND FIFTY
THOUSAND

A hundred and fifty thousand
horses of bituminous rock

along the edges of all things
aglow in God's gaze

flashing in and out of
shade and glare

their hooves and panting breaths
keeping beat with really

each of our hearts
and their black round

eyes of mortal terror

and their round eyes of
devastation

Go to your stables
and wait for your

food to descend

I'm already mourning
for something that has

yet to be taken
away from me

Let me take some
refuge against your

warm breast

Pit me against the world
and I'll still hold on to that

one true thing

without which all things would
dissolve in the

window light like an
envelope of lace doves

suspending the moment of

my death in an

origami figure
unfoldable until

the last moment

My ankles are cold
and it's still summer

How can we let our cat go
who has lived with us

since a kitten for all of
nine years day in and

day out
though she stays in and

isn't let out

My heart will be
torn from my body

when she leaves
if she leaves

I'm convinced of
cat familiars

and she's one of them

Maybe even my
poetry jinn

good in her purrs
bad in her

occasional claws

I *won't* bid her
farewell

9/18

ARAFAT

We stand on earth
full height

among Allah's creatures
head surrounded by

geese encircled by
vultures

gazing unwaveringly at
His central Light

the way the sun holds us all
in its spatial embrace

plants bursting into
Glory at our feet

in the doorway between
worlds

where unicorns nibble

on our hair and

nuzzle our eyebrows

Not a motion lost
nor a hair's breadth of

breath expended
in the time-in without

time-out of our
mortal allotment

on this tightrope
we stand on

between here
where we are

to there
where we will be

where He is
and we are not

and all is perfect
and all is well

white noise in
this world

silver
in the next

9/23

SECOND OPINION

Waiting for second opinion
eye examination

"Macular Degeneration"

Rows of empty chairs in the
waiting room

Something Oz-like behind the
clinic doors

Lots of blue smoke and crystals slowly
revolving in their own

light

Doctors in long white
gowns and pointed hats

and central to all
a huge all-seeing eyeball

on a throne of purple flame

under a diamond dome

Meister Eckhart's words
go through my head

*"The eye through which I
see God is the same*

*eye through which God
sees me"*

a sober thought
that explains our

entire existence in a
phrase

When my name is called will I
evaporate altogether except for my

eyes?
Will sight itself remain supreme?

Will it reach clear to the
empyrean?

Do clouds of God's protective light
surround our seeing?

Do the blind see more than
we do but not of

this world?

We're in God's energy fields
and always have been

from even before our births
and long beyond our

never premature demises

This world and the next in always
perfect synchronization

though this world's opaque
panels keep us for a

time in one visual field
in whatever optical

domain we're in

and if I see zebras in light and
shade in straight and

zigzag lines

and halos around all our
divine heads of

varieties of supernal light

and if God's Face shines
in horizons even

Van Gogh couldn't imagine
would I be bereft?

Our light is lit in this world at the
first light we're given

and if that light dim
isn't it up to Him?

9/29

DEATH WEARS SHOES

Death wears shoes so
tiny it can

get into the smallest of
spaces

a jacket whose cloth is so
vast it can

be thrown around the most
robust among us

a hat so huge
pulled down over its

face the shadow cast
includes everyone

Yet we're oblivious
most of the time

and think it'll arrive
in a perfectly tailored

suit and when we're also
perfectly tailored

An icy black wind
slices the land away from us

A radiant sky of unbearably
blinding light

opens up before and
inside us

And a tiny caterpillar
as white as fog

wiggles across the
windowsill into our

presence

each foot in teeny tiny shoes
and minding its business

does its duty to God's decree
by wriggling its furry

body across our
silhouettes

and taking our substance
the way no sword nor

gun is able to
do as neatly and as

perfectly
in the

wink of an eye

amen

10/2

"IN A SCHOOL OF FISH"

"In a school of fish…"
the professor said

withdrawing his chalk
from the board

*"In a moment within a
moment…"*

the balloonist intoned
as the great globe

rose

*"Certainly dredging the
lake can only…"*

the senator admitted
as the afternoon sun

declined

Yet all these and many

other beginnings

turned suddenly or drifted
off inconclusively

or in fact led to a
barrage of associational

facts and occasional
fictions

about our surprise
universe whose

aspects often seem to be
floating on

nothing more substantial
than language

for its existence

and if we all simply
kept silent

it wouldn't need to
express itself so violently nor

seemingly malevolently

but be itself humbly
sunning itself on a

branch or on a peaceful
beach

listening to the
equally silently

breathing of the sea

under the
implacably endless

silence of the sky

10/12

THE LOQUACIOUSNESS OF NOTHINGNESS

The loquaciousness of nothingness
is drowned out by the

humility of any and
all things

saying their prayers before the
onslaught of annihilation

but in reality it's the
symphony of the

two we experience
and at death it's the

rapturous silence and its
reverberations down

corridors of echo
that awaken us

Nothingness so eloquently
expresses its seemingly

all pervasive and inclusive
sound

while each tinkle and chime
each tweedle and ding-

dong of everything's gongs
clanging all day and

night long
keep us asleep to the

heartbeat of it all

when each beat is the
sonorous

joy of it
all

10/17

INDEX

ABOUT THE AUTHOR

Born in 1940 in Oakland, California, Daniel Abdal-Hayy Moore had his first book of poems, *Dawn Visions*, published by Lawrence Ferlinghetti of City Lights Books, San Francisco, in 1964, and the second in 1972, *Burnt Heart/Ode to the War Dead*. He created and directed *The Floating Lotus Magic Opera Company* in Berkeley, California in the late 60s, and presented two major productions, *The Walls Are Running Blood*, and *Bliss Apocalypse*. He became a Sufi Muslim in 1970, performed the Hajj in 1972, and lived and traveled throughout Morocco, Spain, Algeria and Nigeria, landing in California and publishing *The Desert is the Only Way Out*, and *Chronicles of Akhira* in the early 80s (Zilzal Press). Residing in Philadelphia since 1990, in 1996 he published *The Ramadan Sonnets* (Jusoor/City Lights), and in 2002, *The Blind Beekeeper* (Jusoor/Syracuse University Press). He has been the major editor for a number of works, including The *Burdah* of Shaykh Busiri, translated by Hamza Yusuf, and the poetry of Palestinian poet, Mahmoud Darwish, translated by Munir Akash. He is also widely published on the worldwide web: *The American Muslim, DeenPort*, and his own website among others: www.ecstaticxchange.com. He has been poetry editor for *Seasons Journal, Islamica Magazine*, a 2010 translation by Munir Akash of *State of Siege*, by Mahmoud Darwish (Syracuse University Press), and *The Prayer of the Oppressed*, by Imam Muhammad Nasir al-Dar'i, translated by Hamza Yusuf. In 2011, 2012 and 2014 he was a winner of the Nazim Hikmet Prize for Poetry. In 2013 he won an American Book Award, and in 2013 to 2016 was listed among *The 500 Most Influential Muslims in the World* for his poetry. The Ecstatic Exchange Series is bringing out the body of his works of poetry (a complete list of published works on page 2).

THE WORKS
(Books of poery published and unpublished)

Dawn Visions (City Lights, 1964)
Burnt Heart / Ode to the War Dead (City Lights, 1972)
This Body of Black Light Gone Through the Diamond
    (Fred Stone, Cambridge, Mass, 1965)
On The Streets at Night Alone (1965?)
All Hail the Surgical Lamp (1967)
States of Amazement (1970)

Abdallah Jones and the Disappearing-Dust Caper (The Ecstatic
    Exchange / Crescent Series, 2006)
'Ala ud-Deen and the Magic Lamp (The Ecstatic Exchange /
    Crescent Series, 2011)
The Chronicles of Akhira (1981) (Zilzal Press with Typoglyphs
    by Karl Kempton, 1986; published in *Sparrow on the
    Prophet's Tomb* by The Ecstatic Exchange, 2009)
Mouloud (1984) (A Zilzal Press chapbook, 1995; published
    in *Sparrow on the Prophet's Tomb* by The Ecstatic Exchange,
    2009)
The Crown of Creation (1984) (The Ecstatic Exchange, 2012)
The Look of the Lion (1984)
The Desert is the Only Way Out (completed 4/21/84) (Zilzal
    Press chapbook, 1985)
Atomic Dance (1984) (am here books, 1988)
Outlandish Tales (1984)
Awake as Never Before (12/26/84) (Zilzal Press chapbook,
    1993)
Glorious Intervals (1/1/85) (Zilzal Press chapbook)
Long Days on Earth/Book I (1/28 – 8/30/85)
Long Days on Earth/Book II (Hayy Ibn Yaqzan)
Long Days on Earth/Book III (1/22/86)
Long Days on Earth/Book IV (1986)

You Open a Door and it's a Starry Night (10/29/97 –
    5/23/98) (The Ecstatic Exchange, 2009)

Salt Prayers (5/29 – 10/24/98) (The Ecstatic Exchange, 2005)

Some (10/25/98 – 4/25/99) (published by The Ecstatic Exchange,
    2014)

Flight to Egypt (5/1 – 5/16/99)

I Imagine a Lion (5/21 – 11/15/99) (The Ecstatic Exchange,
    2006)

Millennial Prognostications (11/25/99 – 2/2/2000) (The Ecstatic
    Exchange, 2009)

Shaking the Quicksilver Pool (2/4 – 10/8/2000) (The Ecstatic
    Exchange, 2009)

Blood Songs (10/9/2000 – 4/3/2001) (The Ecstatic Exchange,
    2012)

The Music Space (4/10 – 9/16/2001) (The Ecstatic Exchange,
    2007)

Where Death Goes (9/20/2001 – 5/1/2002) (The Ecstatic
    Exchange, 2009)

The Flame of Transformation Turns to Light (99 Ghazals
    Written in English) (5/14 – 8/21/2002) (The Ecstatic
    Exchange, 2007)

Through Rose-Colored Glasses (7/22/2002 – 1/15/2003)
    (The Ecstatic Exchange, 2007)

Psalms for the Broken-Hearted (1/22 – 5/25/2003) (The Ecstatic
    Exchange, 2006)

Hoopoe's Argument (5/27 – 9/18/03)

Love is a Letter Burning in a High Wind (9/21 – 11/6/2003)
    (The Ecstatic Exchange, 2006)

Laughing Buddha/Weeping Sufi (11/7/2003 – 1/10/2004)
    (The Ecstatic Exchange, 2005)

Mars and Beyond (1/20 – 3/29/2004) (The Ecstatic Exchange,
    2005)

Underwater Galaxies (4/5 – 7/21/2004) (The Ecstatic Exchange,
    2007)

Cooked Oranges (7/23/2004 – 1/24/2005 (The Ecstatic
    Exchange, 2007)

Holiday from the Perfect Crime (1/25 – 6/11/2005) (The Ecstatic Exchange, 2011)

Stories Too Fiery to Sing Too Watery to Whisper (6/13 – 10/24/200? (The Ecstatic Exchange, 2014)

Coattails of the Saint (10/26/2005 – 5/10/2006) (The Ecstatic Exchange, 2006)

In the Realm of Neither (5/14/2006 – 11/12/06) (The Ecstatic Exchange, 2008)

Invention of the Wheel (11/13/06 – 6/10/07) (The Ecstatic Exchange, 2010)

The Sound of Geese Over the House (6/15 – 11/4/07) (The Ecstatic Exchange, 2015)

The Fire Eater's Lunchbreak (11/11/07 – 5/19/2008) (The Ecstatic Exchange, 2008)

Sparks Off the Main Strike (5/24/2008 – 1/10/2009) (The Ecstatic Exchange, 2010)

Stretched Out on Amethysts (1/13 – 9/17/2009) (The Ecstatic Exchange, 2010)

The Throne Perpendicular to All that is Horizontal (9/18/09 – 1/25/10) (The Ecstatic Exchange, 2014)

In Constant Incandescence (2/10 – 8/13/10) (The Ecstatic Exchange, 2011)

The Caged Bear Spies the Angel (8/30/10 – 3/6/11) (The Ecstatic Exchange, 2010)

This Light Slants Upward (3/7 – 10/13/11)

Ramadan is Burnished Sunlight (part of *This Light Slants Upward*, published separately by The Ecstatic Exchange, 2011)

The Match That Becomes a Conflagration (10/14/11– 5/9/12)

Down at the Deep End (5/10 – 8/3/12) (The Ecstatic Exchange, 2012)

Next Life (8/9/12 – 2/12/13) (The Ecstatic Exchange, 2013)

The Soul's Home (2/13 – 10/8/13) (The Ecstatic Exchange, 2014)

Eternity Shimmers & Time Holds its Breath (10/10/13 – 1/27/14) (The Ecstatic Exchange, 2014)

He Comes Running (part of *Eternity Shimmers*, published as an Ecstatic Exchange Chapbook, 2014)

www.ingramcontent.com/pod-product-compliance
Lightning Source LLC
Chambersburg PA
CBHW071420090426
42737CB00011B/1518